REACTJS ESSENTIALS: LEARN THE BASICS IN A WEEKEND

Deepesh Rastogi

Table of Contents

Introduction

- Welcome to ReactJS Essentials
- How to Use This Book

Chapter 1: Getting Started with React

- What is React?
- History and Evolution of React
- Key Features of React
- Setting Up Your Development Environment

Chapter 2: Core Concepts of React

- Components and Props
- State and Lifecycle
- Handling Events
- Conditional Rendering

Chapter 3: Working with Lists and Forms

- Rendering Lists in React
- Managing Forms and User Input

- Controlled vs. Uncontrolled Components

Chapter 4: Component Composition

- Understanding Component Hierarchy
- Reusable Components and Props
- Composition vs. Inheritance

Chapter 5: Styling in React

- CSS in JS: Styled Components
- Inline Styles vs. Stylesheets
- Responsive Design with React

Chapter 6: State Management

- Introduction to State Management
- Context API Overview
- Introduction to Redux

Chapter 7: React Router

- Understanding Single Page Applications (SPAs)
- Setting Up React Router
- Navigation and Route Parameters

Chapter 8: Fetching Data

- Introduction to API Calls

- Using Fetch and Axios
- Handling Async Operations in React

Chapter 9: Testing React Applications

- Importance of Testing
- Introduction to Jest and React Testing Library
- Writing Unit Tests for Components

Chapter 10: Building and Deploying Your Application

- Preparing for Production
- Building Your React Application
- Deployment Options

Summary

- Recap of Key Concepts
- Next Steps in Your React Journey

Additional Resources

- Recommended Books and Courses
- Online Communities and Forums

Introduction

Welcome to ReactJS Essentials: Learn the Basics in a Weekend! This book is designed for beginners eager to dive into the world of React, a powerful JavaScript library for building user interfaces. Whether you're a developer looking to enhance your skill set or a newcomer to web development, this guide will equip you with essential knowledge to get started with React in just two days.

In the following chapters, we'll cover the core concepts of React, including components, state management, and routing. You'll learn how to create dynamic and interactive web applications using practical examples and hands-on exercises. Each chapter is structured to build upon the previous one, ensuring a smooth learning curve.

Don't hesitate to revisit chapters as needed, and consider joining online communities to enhance your learning experience. By the end of this journey, you'll have a solid foundation in React, ready to tackle more advanced topics and build your own applications. **Let's get started!**

Chapter 1: Getting Started with React

What is React?

React is an open-source JavaScript library developed for building user interfaces, particularly single-page applications where a dynamic and responsive user experience is paramount. It allows developers to create large web applications that can change data without reloading the entire page, leading to a smoother user experience. React operates on a component-based architecture, where the UI is divided into reusable components, each managing its own state. This modular approach makes it easier to develop, maintain, and test applications, as each component can be developed in isolation.

React utilizes a declarative programming model, which means developers describe what the UI should look like for any given state, and React takes care of updating and rendering the components efficiently when the state changes. This enhances productivity, as developers can focus on building components rather than managing the complex DOM manipulations.

JSX: A Syntax Extension

One of the standout features of React is JSX (JavaScript XML), a syntax extension that allows developers to write HTML-like code within JavaScript. JSX simplifies the process of creating React elements and enhances readability. For instance, instead of using JavaScript's `createElement` method to create UI components, developers can write:

const element = <h1>Hello, World!</h1>;

This combination of JavaScript and HTML in JSX streamlines the development process and makes it intuitive for those familiar with HTML.

History and Evolution of React

React was developed by Facebook in 2011 to address challenges in building user interfaces for large-scale applications. Its initial release was kept private until it was open-sourced in May 2013. Since then, it has undergone significant evolution, driven by both internal needs at Facebook and community contributions.

Key Milestones in React's Evolution:

1. **2013: Open Source Release**
   The release of React as an open-source library marked its entry into the developer community. The initial version included essential features such as the virtual DOM and component lifecycle methods.
2. **2015: Introduction of React Router**
   React Router emerged as a solution for handling routing in single-page applications, allowing developers to manage navigation without reloading the page.
3. **2016: React 15**
   This version introduced significant performance improvements and enhancements to server-side rendering capabilities, making React more robust for production use.
4. **2017: Introduction of Hooks**
   The release of React 16.8 brought hooks to the library, allowing developers to use state and other React features without writing classes. This was a game-changer, simplifying component logic and promoting functional programming styles in React development.
5. **Ongoing Updates**
   React continues to evolve, with frequent updates that introduce new features, performance optimizations, and enhancements based on user feedback. The

community around React is vibrant, contributing to a rich ecosystem of libraries, tools, and resources.

Key Features of React

React offers several key features that contribute to its popularity among developers:

1. Component-Based Architecture

At the core of React is its component-based architecture, which promotes reusability and modularity. Each component encapsulates its own logic, rendering, and state, making it easier to manage complex UIs by breaking them into smaller, manageable pieces. This also enhances code maintainability, as changes to one component have minimal impact on others.

2. Virtual DOM

React uses a virtual DOM to optimize rendering. When the state of a component changes, React first updates the virtual DOM, a lightweight representation of the actual DOM. It then compares the virtual DOM with the real DOM to determine the most efficient way to update the UI. This minimizes direct DOM manipulations, leading to improved performance and a more responsive user experience.

3. Unidirectional Data Flow

In React, data flows in a single direction, from parent components to child components. This unidirectional data flow simplifies the management of data and state, making it easier to understand how data changes impact the UI. It also facilitates debugging and testing, as developers can trace data changes throughout the component hierarchy.

4. Declarative Syntax

React's declarative syntax allows developers to describe how the UI should look for any given state, rather than specifying step-by-step instructions for updating the UI. This approach reduces the complexity of the code and improves readability. Developers can focus on what the UI should display based on the current state, leading to cleaner and more maintainable code.

5. Hooks

With the introduction of hooks, React allows developers to manage state and side effects in functional components. Hooks like `useState`, `useEffect`, and custom hooks enable a more functional programming approach, promoting cleaner and more reusable code without the need for class-based components.

6. Rich Ecosystem

React has a vibrant ecosystem of libraries and tools that complement its core functionalities. Libraries like Redux for state management, React Router for routing, and Styled Components for styling enhance the development experience and expand the capabilities of React applications.

Setting Up Your Development Environment

To get started with React, you'll need to set up your development environment. Here's a step-by-step guide to help you through the process:

1. Install Node.js and npm

React development requires Node.js, a JavaScript runtime that allows you to run JavaScript on the server side. npm (Node Package Manager) comes bundled with Node.js and is used to install libraries and manage dependencies. You can download Node.js from the official website and follow the installation instructions.

2. Create a New React Application

The easiest way to set up a new React project is by using Create React App, a command-line tool that sets up everything you need for a React application.

Open your terminal or command prompt and run the following command:

```
cd my-app
```

4. Start the Development Server

To start the development server and see your React application in action, run:

npm start

This command will open your default web browser and display your new React application at `http://localhost:3000`. The development server supports hot reloading, meaning any changes you make to the code will automatically reflect in the browser without needing a manual refresh.

5. Explore the Project Structure

Once your application is running, take a moment to explore the project structure created by Create React App. Key folders and files include:

- `src/`: This folder contains your React components, styles, and other source files.
- `public/`: This folder holds static files like the HTML template and images.

- `package.json`: This file lists your project's dependencies and scripts.

6. Install Additional Libraries (Optional)

As you build your application, you may want to incorporate additional libraries for routing, state management, or styling. Use npm to install any required libraries. For example, to install React Router, run:

npm install react-router-dom

Conclusion

With React set up and your development environment ready, you're now equipped to start building dynamic user interfaces. In the following chapters, you'll dive deeper into React's core concepts, learn about component creation and management, and explore best practices for building efficient applications. Embrace the modularity and flexibility of React, and get ready to create engaging user experiences!

Chapter 2: Core Concepts of React

In this chapter, we will explore the fundamental concepts of React that form the backbone of any React application. Understanding components, props, state, lifecycle methods, event handling, and conditional rendering will provide you with the essential tools to build dynamic and interactive user interfaces.

Components and Props

What are Components?

Components are the building blocks of any React application. A component is a self-contained piece of code that represents a part of the user interface. Components can be classified into two types: **Class Components** and **Functional Components**.

- **Class Components**: These are ES6 classes that extend the `React.Component` class. They can hold state and have lifecycle methods. A class component typically looks like this:

```
class MyComponent extends React.Component {
    render() {
```

```
        return <h1>Hello, World!</h1>;

    }

}
```

Functional Components: These are simpler components defined as JavaScript functions. They are easier to read and test, and since the introduction of hooks in React 16.8, functional components can also manage state and lifecycle events. A functional component looks like this:

```
function MyComponent() {

    return <h1>Hello, World!</h1>;

}
```

What are Props?

Props (short for properties) are a way to pass data from one component to another. They allow components to be dynamic and reusable. Props are read-only; a child component cannot modify the props it receives from its parent.

Here's an example of how to use props:

```
function Greeting(props) {

    return <h1>Hello, {props.name}!</h1>;

}
```

```
function App() {
  return <Greeting name="Alice" />;
}
```

In this example, the `Greeting` component receives a prop called `name`, which is used to render a personalized message.

State and Lifecycle

Understanding State

State is a built-in object that allows components to create and manage their own data. Unlike props, state is mutable; it can change over time, usually in response to user actions. When the state of a component changes, React automatically re-renders that component to reflect the new state.

Here's how to define and use state in a class component:

```
class Counter extends React.Component {
  constructor(props) {
    super(props);
```

```
    this.state = { count: 0 };
}

increment = () => {
    this.setState({ count: this.state.count + 1 });
};

render() {
    return (
        <div>
            <h1>Count: {this.state.count}</h1>
            <button onClick={this.increment}>Increment</button>
        </div>
    );
}
}
```

In the `Counter` component, the state holds a `count` value that can be updated through the `increment` method.

Lifecycle Methods

Lifecycle methods are special methods that allow you to hook into specific points in a component's life: when it mounts, updates, or unmounts. Common lifecycle methods include:

componentDidMount(): Called after the component is mounted. Useful for fetching data.

componentDidUpdate(prevProps, prevState): Called after the component updates. Useful for responding to prop or state changes.

componentWillUnmount(): Called before the component unmounts. Useful for cleanup tasks, such as canceling API calls or timers.

Example of a lifecycle method in a class component:

```
class FetchData extends React.Component {
  constructor(props) {
    super(props);
    this.state = { data: null };
  }

  componentDidMount() {
    fetch("https://api.example.com/data")
      .then(response => response.json())
```

```
      .then(data => this.setState({ data }));
  }

  render() {
    return (
      <div>
        {this.state.data ? <p>{this.state.data}</p> : <p>Loading...</p>}
      </div>
    );
  }
}
```

In this example, data is fetched when the component mounts, and the component re-renders when the data is available.

Handling Events

React simplifies event handling by providing a consistent and straightforward API. Events in React are handled using camelCase syntax rather than lowercase. For example, onClick instead of onclick.

Adding Event Handlers

To handle events in React, you typically define a function and pass it as a prop to the component. Here's a simple example:

```
class Button extends React.Component {
  handleClick = () => {
    alert("Button clicked!");
  };
  render() {
    return <button onClick={this.handleClick}>Click Me</button>;
  }
}
```

In this example, clicking the button triggers the handleClick method, displaying an alert.

Passing Arguments to Event Handlers

You can also pass arguments to event handlers by using an arrow function. For example:

```
class Greeting extends React.Component {
  handleGreet = (name) => {
    alert(`Hello, ${name}!`);
```

```
  };
  render() {
    return <button onClick={() =>
this.handleGreet("Alice")}>Greet</button>;
  }
}
```

This pattern allows you to call the `handleGreet` function with a specific argument when the button is clicked.

Conditional Rendering

Conditional rendering in React enables you to display different UI elements based on the state or props. This can be achieved using JavaScript operators like `if`, `ternary operator`, or logical `&&`.

Using If Statements

You can use regular `if` statements to conditionally render components:

```
class Toggle extends React.Component {
  constructor(props) {
```

```
    super(props);
    this.state = { isOn: false };
  }


  toggle = () => {
    this.setState(prevState => ({ isOn: !prevState.isOn
}));
  };


  render() {
    if (this.state.isOn) {
      return <h1>The switch is ON</h1>;
    }
    return <h1>The switch is OFF</h1>;
  }
}
```

Using the Ternary Operator

The ternary operator is a concise way to handle conditional rendering:

class UserGreeting extends React.Component {

```
  render() {
    const isLoggedIn = this.props.isLoggedIn;
    return (
      <h1>{isLoggedIn ? "Welcome back!" : "Please sign up."}</h1>
    );
  }
}
```

Using Logical AND (&&)

The logical AND operator can also be used for conditional rendering:

```
class Notification extends React.Component {
  render() {
    const messages = this.props.messages;
    return (
      <div>
        {messages.length > 0 && <h2>You have {messages.length} new messages!</h2>}
      </div>
    );
```

```
    }
}
```

In this example, the notification message is displayed only if there are new messages.

Conclusion

Understanding the core concepts of React—components, props, state, lifecycle methods, event handling, and conditional rendering—is essential for building dynamic and interactive web applications. By leveraging these concepts, you can create reusable components that effectively manage their own data and respond to user interactions.

As you progress in your React journey, keep experimenting with these concepts to build more complex applications. In the next chapters, you'll explore more advanced topics, including component composition, styling, and state management, further enhancing your React development skills.

Chapter 3: Working with Lists and Forms

In modern web development, React has become a popular choice due to its component-based architecture and ability to handle complex user interfaces. Two of the most essential aspects of building dynamic applications with React are managing lists and forms. This chapter provides an in-depth exploration of rendering lists, managing user input through forms, and the critical distinction between controlled and uncontrolled components.

Rendering Lists in React

Introduction to Lists

Lists are a fundamental part of most web applications, as they allow for the presentation of collections of data. In React, rendering lists efficiently is vital for performance and user experience. React provides a simple yet powerful way to render lists using the `map()` function, which iterates over an array and returns a new array populated with React elements.

Basic List Rendering

To illustrate how to render lists, consider a simple example where we want to display a list of fruits:

```
const fruits = ['Apple', 'Banana', 'Cherry'];
function FruitList() {
  return (
    <ul>
      {fruits.map((fruit, index) => (
        <li key={index}>{fruit}</li>
      ))}
    </ul>
  );
}
```

In this `FruitList` component, we utilize the `map()` function to iterate over the `fruits` array. Each fruit is rendered as a list item (`<li>`), and it's crucial to provide a unique `key` prop. The `key` prop is essential for React's reconciliation process, which allows React to optimize rendering by identifying which items have changed, been added, or removed.

Dynamic Lists with State

In real-world applications, lists are often dynamic and can change in response to user actions. React's state management allows us to update lists easily.

Below is an example of a dynamic list that allows users to add items:

```jsx
import React, { useState } from 'react';

function DynamicFruitList() {

  const [fruits, setFruits] = useState(['Apple', 'Banana', 'Cherry']);

  const [inputValue, setInputValue] = useState('');

  const addFruit = () => {

    if (inputValue.trim()) {

      setFruits([...fruits, inputValue]);

      setInputValue('');

    }

  };

  return (

    <div>

      <input

        type="text"

        value={inputValue}

        onChange={(e) => setInputValue(e.target.value)}

      />

      <button onClick={addFruit}>Add Fruit</button>
```

```
    <ul>
      {fruits.map((fruit, index) => (
        <li key={index}>{fruit}</li>
      ))}
    </ul>
  </div>
  );
}
```

In `DynamicFruitList`, we manage the list of fruits and the input value with React's `useState` hook. When the user types in the input box, the `inputValue` state updates. Upon clicking the "Add Fruit" button, the `addFruit` function updates the `fruits` array and resets the input field. This demonstrates how React automatically re-renders the component whenever the state changes.

Handling Complex Lists

Sometimes, lists contain more complex data structures, such as objects. For example, consider a list of user profiles:

```
const users = [
  { id: 1, name: 'Alice', age: 30 },
  { id: 2, name: 'Bob', age: 25 },
  { id: 3, name: 'Charlie', age: 35 },
];
function UserList() {
  return (
    <ul>
      {users.map((user) => (
        <li key={user.id}>
          {user.name} is {user.age} years old.
        </li>
      ))}
    </ul>
  );
}
```

In this `UserList` example, each user is represented by an object. By using a unique property (in this case, `id`) as the `key`, we ensure that React can efficiently manage changes in the list.

List Manipulation Techniques

Managing lists often requires operations such as adding, removing, or updating items. Here's how to implement these features in a simple user interface:

```
import React, { useState } from 'react';

function ManageUsers() {

  const [users, setUsers] = useState([

    { id: 1, name: 'Alice', age: 30 },

    { id: 2, name: 'Bob', age: 25 },

  ]);

  const [name, setName] = useState('');

  const [age, setAge] = useState('');

  const addUser = () => {

    if (name.trim() && age.trim()) {
```

```jsx
    setUsers([...users, { id: Date.now(), name, age: parseInt(age) }]);

    setName("");

    setAge("");

  }
};

const removeUser = (id) => {

  setUsers(users.filter(user => user.id !== id));

};

return (

  <div>

    <input

      type="text"

      placeholder="Name"

      value={name}

      onChange={(e) => setName(e.target.value)}

    />
```

```jsx
<input
  type="number"
  placeholder="Age"
  value={age}
  onChange={(e) => setAge(e.target.value)}
/>
<button onClick={addUser}>Add User</button>
<ul>
  {users.map((user) => (
    <li key={user.id}>
      {user.name} ({user.age})
      <button onClick={() => removeUser(user.id)}>Remove</button>
    </li>
  ))}
</ul>
```

```
    </div>
  );
}
```

In `ManageUsers`, we provide a form to add new users and a button to remove existing ones. The `removeUser` function demonstrates how to filter the users list based on the user's unique `id`. This example highlights the power of React's state management to create dynamic user interfaces.

Managing Forms and User Input

Importance of Forms

Forms are central to user interaction in web applications, enabling users to input data that can be submitted or processed. React provides robust mechanisms for handling forms, allowing developers to manage form state and validation efficiently.

Controlled Components

In a controlled component, the form input values are controlled by the component's state. This means that the state is the single source of truth for form data. Here's a simple example of a controlled form:

```jsx
import React, { useState } from 'react';
function ControlledForm() {
  const [name, setName] = useState("");
  const [email, setEmail] = useState("");
  const handleSubmit = (e) => {
    e.preventDefault();
    alert(`Name: ${name}, Email: ${email}`);
    setName("");
    setEmail("");
  };
  return (
    <form onSubmit={handleSubmit}>
      <label>
        Name:
        <input
          type="text"
```

```jsx
        value={name}
        onChange={(e) => setName(e.target.value)}
      />
    </label>
    <label>
      Email:
      <input
        type="email"
        value={email}
        onChange={(e) => setEmail(e.target.value)}
      />
    </label>
    <button type="submit">Submit</button>
  </form>
);
}
```

In the `ControlledForm`, the input fields for name and email are bound to the state variables. The `handleSubmit` function prevents the default form submission, allowing us to process the data (in this case, displaying an alert). By updating the state with `setName` and `setEmail`, the inputs reflect the latest values, ensuring the UI is in sync with the underlying data.

Uncontrolled Components

In some scenarios, using uncontrolled components may be more suitable, particularly when dealing with complex forms or integrating with third-party libraries. Uncontrolled components do not store their input state in React but rather rely on the DOM itself.

Here's an example of an uncontrolled form:

```
import React, { useRef } from 'react';

function UncontrolledForm() {

  const nameRef = useRef();

  const emailRef = useRef();

  const handleSubmit = (e) => {

    e.preventDefault();
```

```jsx
    alert(`Name: ${nameRef.current.value}, Email: ${emailRef.current.value}`);
  };

  return (
    <form onSubmit={handleSubmit}>
      <label>
        Name:
        <input type="text" ref={nameRef} />
      </label>
      <label>
        Email:
        <input type="email" ref={emailRef} />
      </label>
      <button type="submit">Submit</button>
    </form>
  );
}
```

In the `UncontrolledForm`, we use the `useRef` hook to create references for the input fields. Instead of managing state, we access the input values directly from the DOM upon form submission. This approach can simplify handling forms, particularly when using libraries that manipulate the DOM directly.

When to Use Controlled vs. Uncontrolled Components

Deciding whether to use controlled or uncontrolled components depends on the specific needs of your application:

- **Controlled Components**: Use controlled components when you need complete control over form data. This is especially useful when implementing complex validation, conditional rendering based on input values, or when needing to synchronize form data with other parts of the application state. Controlled components are generally preferred for their predictability and ease of testing.
- **Uncontrolled Components**: Uncontrolled components can be beneficial in cases where you want to reduce the overhead of managing form state in React. They can also be advantageous when integrating with non-React libraries that expect direct access to

the DOM, such as when using a jQuery plugin for form handling.

Validating Forms

Form validation is an essential aspect of user input management. It ensures that users provide the expected data format before submission. Here's how you can implement basic validation in a controlled component:

import React, { useState } from 'react';

function ValidatedForm() {

　const [name, setName] = useState('');

　const [error, setError] = useState('');

　const handleSubmit = (e) => {

　　e.preventDefault();

　　if (name.trim() === '') {

　　　setError('Name is required.');

　　} else {

　　　setError('');

　　　alert(`Name: ${name}`);

```
      setName('');
    }
  };

  return (
    <form onSubmit={handleSubmit}>
      <label> Name:
        <input type="text"
          value={name}
          onChange={(e) => setName(e.target.value)}
        />
      </label>
      {error && <p style={{ color: 'red' }}>{error}</p>}
      <button type="submit">Submit</button>
    </form>
  );
}
```

In the `ValidatedForm`, we introduce a simple validation check to ensure that the name field is not empty. If validation fails, an error message is displayed, preventing form submission. This pattern can be expanded to include more complex validations based on requirements.

Conclusion

In this chapter, we explored the essential concepts of working with lists and forms in React. Rendering lists using the `map()` function, managing dynamic state for lists, and understanding how to effectively handle forms through controlled and uncontrolled components are crucial skills for any React developer.

We also examined how to manage user input, implement form validation, and make informed decisions about when to use controlled versus uncontrolled components. Mastering these topics is vital for building robust, user-friendly applications that can effectively handle user data and provide seamless interaction experiences. As you continue to work with React, these foundational skills will empower you to create dynamic and responsive user interfaces, ultimately enhancing the overall user experience.

Chapter 4: Component Composition

In React, component composition is a fundamental concept that allows developers to build complex user interfaces by combining simpler components. This chapter will delve into three key aspects of component composition: understanding component hierarchy, creating reusable components using props, and the distinction between composition and inheritance.

Understanding Component Hierarchy

What is Component Hierarchy?

Component hierarchy refers to the structure in which components are organized within a React application. Every React application consists of a tree of components, where each component can contain other components. This hierarchy is essential for managing the application's UI and behavior, as it defines how components communicate and share data.

Root Component

At the top of the hierarchy is the root component, often called `App`. This component serves as the entry point for the entire application. From here, other components can be nested within the root component, creating a structured and organized codebase. For example:

```
function App() {
  return (
    <div>
      <Header />
      <MainContent />
      <Footer />
    </div>
  );
}
```

In this `App` component, `Header`, `MainContent`, and `Footer` are child components that make up the application's layout. This parent-child relationship allows data and functions to flow from the parent to its children through props, enabling a unidirectional data flow that React is known for.

Managing State in Hierarchies

In complex applications, managing state becomes crucial. Typically, the component at the top of the hierarchy holds the state that needs to be shared among its children. This state can be passed down as props. For example:

```
function App() {
  const [user, setUser] = useState(null);

  return (
    <div>
      <Header user={user} />
      <MainContent user={user} setUser={setUser} />
      <Footer />
    </div>
  );
}
```

In this example, the `App` component holds the user state and passes it to `Header` and `MainContent`. This allows both components to access and interact with the shared state while maintaining a clean and manageable hierarchy.

Reusable Components and Props

What are Reusable Components?

Reusable components are the building blocks of React applications. They are designed to be used in multiple places throughout the application, reducing code duplication and enhancing maintainability. A reusable component is typically generic enough to handle various scenarios while remaining focused on a specific task.

Creating Reusable Components

To create a reusable component, consider what props it might need to function in different contexts. For example, a `Button` component can be made reusable by allowing it to accept various props:

function Button({ label, onClick, color }) {

  return (

    <button style={{ backgroundColor: color }} onClick={onClick}>

      {label} </button>);

}

In this `Button` component, the `label`, `onClick`, and `color` props allow it to be used flexibly in different situations. For instance:

```
function App() {

  const handleClick = () => alert('Button clicked!');


  return (

    <div>

      <Button label="Submit" onClick={handleClick} color="blue" />

      <Button label="Cancel" onClick={handleClick} color="red" />

    </div>

  );

}
```

Here, the `Button` component is reused with different labels and colors, demonstrating how reusable components can simplify the codebase and enhance consistency across the application.

Prop Types and Default Props

To ensure components are used correctly, React provides tools such as `propTypes` and default props. Using `propTypes`, you can specify the expected data types for props:

import PropTypes from 'prop-types';

Button.propTypes = {

  label: PropTypes.string.isRequired,

  onClick: PropTypes.func.isRequired,

  color: PropTypes.string,

};

Button.defaultProps = {

  color: 'gray', // Default color if none is provided

};

This helps in catching bugs and providing clearer documentation for how to use components.

Composition vs. Inheritance

Understanding Composition

In React, composition is the preferred method for creating components that combine functionality and behavior. Instead of relying on inheritance (which can lead to complicated hierarchies), React encourages developers to compose components together.

Example of Composition

Consider a scenario where you have a `Card` component that should display content with a header and a footer:

```
function Card({ header, footer, children }) {
  return (
    <div className="card">
      <h2>{header}</h2>  <div>{children}</div>
      <footer>{footer}</footer>
    </div>
  );
}
```

The `Card` component can now be composed with other components:

```
function App() {

  return (

    <Card header="Welcome" footer="Thank you for visiting">

      <p>This is the main content of the card.</p>

    </Card>

  );

}
```

In this example, `children` allows you to pass any JSX content inside the `Card`, promoting a flexible and reusable design.

Advantages of Composition

1. **Flexibility**: Composition allows for the combination of various components to create new functionalities without altering existing components.
2. **Separation of Concerns**: Each component can focus on a specific responsibility, making the code easier to maintain and understand.

3. **Easier Testing**: Individual components can be tested in isolation, leading to more robust applications.

Understanding Inheritance

While inheritance is a common paradigm in traditional object-oriented programming, it is generally discouraged in React for several reasons:

1. **Complexity**: Inheritance can lead to complicated class hierarchies, making code difficult to understand and manage.
2. **Tight Coupling**: Inherited components are tightly coupled, meaning changes in a parent class can inadvertently affect child classes, leading to bugs.
3. **Limited Flexibility**: Inheritance restricts component reusability, as subclasses often need to inherit a specific structure and behavior from their parent.

Conclusion

In React, component composition is a powerful technique that enables developers to build complex user interfaces from simple, reusable components. By understanding component hierarchy, creating reusable components using props, and favoring composition over inheritance, developers can create maintainable, scalable applications. The principles outlined in this chapter are foundational for effective React development, fostering a clear structure and enhancing code reusability. As you continue to build React applications, mastering component composition will greatly improve your development efficiency and code quality.

Chapter 5: Styling in React

Styling is a crucial aspect of web development, and in React, it can be approached in various ways. This chapter explores different methods for styling React components, focusing on CSS-in-JS using styled components, the comparison between inline styles and traditional stylesheets, and techniques for implementing responsive design.

CSS in JS: Styled Components

Introduction to CSS-in-JS

CSS-in-JS is a modern approach that allows developers to write CSS directly within JavaScript files. This method integrates styles with the component logic, enhancing maintainability and modularity. One of the most popular libraries for implementing CSS-in-JS is **Styled Components**.

What are Styled Components?

Styled Components is a library that utilizes tagged template literals to create styled React components. It allows developers to define their styles in the same file as their components, improving readability and organization. Here's a basic example:

```jsx
import styled from 'styled-components';

const Button = styled.button`
  background-color: blue;
  color: white;
  border: none;
  padding: 10px 20px;
  border-radius: 5px;
  cursor: pointer;
  &:hover {
    background-color: darkblue;
  }
`;

function App() {
  return (
    <div>
      <Button>Click Me</Button>
    </div>
  );
}
```

In this example, the `Button` component is styled using the `styled.button` syntax. The styles are encapsulated within the component, ensuring that they won't conflict with other styles in the application. Additionally, using pseudo-classes like `&:hover` allows for dynamic styling based on user interactions.

Benefits of Styled Components

1. **Scoped Styles**: Styles are scoped to the component, preventing global namespace pollution and conflicts.
2. **Dynamic Styling**: Styled Components can accept props, allowing for dynamic styling based on the component's state or external parameters.
3. **Theming**: Styled Components support theming, enabling developers to create consistent design systems across their applications easily.

Example of Dynamic Styling

Here's an example that demonstrates how to use props for dynamic styling:

```
const Button = styled.button`
  background-color: ${(props) => (props.primary ? 'blue' : 'gray')};
  color: white;
```

```
  padding: 10px 20px;

  border: none;

  border-radius: 5px;
`;


function App() {
  return (
    <div>
      <Button primary>Primary Button</Button>
      <Button>Secondary Button</Button>
    </div>
  );
}
```

In this example, the `Button` component changes its background color based on the `primary` prop, showcasing the flexibility of styled components.

Inline Styles vs. Stylesheets

Inline Styles

Inline styles are a method of applying CSS directly to elements using the `style` attribute. In React, this attribute accepts a JavaScript object where the property names are camelCased versions of the CSS property names.

Example of Inline Styles:

```
function App() {
  const buttonStyle = {
    backgroundColor: 'blue',
    color: 'white',
    padding: '10px 20px',
    border: 'none',
    borderRadius: '5px',
    cursor: 'pointer',
  };

  return (
    <button style={buttonStyle}>Click Me</button>
  );
}
```

Advantages of Inline Styles

1. **Scoped Styles**: Similar to CSS-in-JS, inline styles are scoped to the component, preventing conflicts.
2. **Dynamic Styles**: Inline styles can easily incorporate JavaScript logic, making it simple to create styles based on state or props.

Disadvantages of Inline Styles

1. **Limited Features**: Inline styles do not support features like pseudo-classes (`:hover`, `:focus`, etc.) or media queries.
2. **Performance**: Applying styles inline can lead to performance issues, as styles are recalculated on every render.

Traditional Stylesheets

Traditional stylesheets involve writing CSS in separate `.css` files, which are then imported into the component files. This approach is familiar and widely used but comes with its own set of advantages and challenges.

Example of a Stylesheet:

```
/* styles.css */

.button {
```

```
  background-color: blue;
  color: white;
  padding: 10px 20px;
  border: none;
  border-radius: 5px;
  cursor: pointer;
}
```

```
import './styles.css';

function App() {
  return (
    <button className="button">Click Me</button>
  );
}
```

Advantages of Stylesheets

1. **Global Styles**: Stylesheets allow for the definition of global styles that can be applied across multiple components.

2. **CSS Features**: Stylesheets support all CSS features, including media queries, animations, and pseudo-classes.

Disadvantages of Stylesheets

1. **Namespace Pollution**: Global styles can lead to conflicts, especially in larger applications where multiple components may use the same class names.
2. **Less Modularity**: Styles are separated from components, which can make it harder to understand the relationship between styles and the components they affect.

Responsive Design with React

Importance of Responsive Design

Responsive design ensures that applications look and function well on a variety of devices, from desktops to mobile phones. With React, there are several strategies for implementing responsive design effectively.

CSS Media Queries

One common approach to achieving responsive design is using CSS media queries. Media queries allow you to apply different styles based on the viewport size.

Example of Media Queries:

/* styles.css */

.button {

  padding: 10px 20px;

}

@media (max-width: 600px) {

  .button {

    padding: 5px 10px;

  }

}

In this example, the button's padding adjusts based on the viewport width, ensuring a better experience on smaller screens.

CSS Frameworks

Another option is to use CSS frameworks like Bootstrap or Tailwind CSS. These frameworks come with pre-defined responsive classes, making it easy to build responsive layouts quickly.

Example using Bootstrap:

```
import 'bootstrap/dist/css/bootstrap.min.css';


function App() {
  return (
    <button className="btn btn-primary">Click Me</button>
  );
}
```

With Bootstrap, classes like `btn` and `btn-primary` automatically apply responsive styles, simplifying the process of creating a responsive design.

Responsive Design with Flexbox and Grid

Flexbox and CSS Grid are powerful layout systems that can help create responsive designs more easily. These layout models allow developers to control the arrangement and alignment of components efficiently.

Example using Flexbox:

```css
.container {
  display: flex;
  flex-direction: row;
  justify-content: space-between;
}


.item {
  flex: 1; /* Grow to fill space */
}
```

In this example, a flex container arranges its items in a row, automatically adjusting their widths based on available space.

React Responsive Libraries

There are also libraries specifically designed to help manage responsive design in React, such as `react-responsive` or `react-media`. These libraries allow you to conditionally render components based on screen size.

Example with `react-responsive`:

```
import { useMediaQuery } from 'react-responsive';

function App() {

  const isMobile = useMediaQuery({ query: '(max-width: 600px)' });


  return (
    <div>
      {isMobile ? (
        <h1>Mobile View</h1>
      ) : (
        <h1>Desktop View</h1>
      )}
    </div>
  );
}
```

In this example, the `useMediaQuery` hook determines the viewport size, enabling different content to be displayed for mobile and desktop users.

Conclusion

Styling in React offers numerous approaches, from CSS-in-JS with libraries like Styled Components to traditional stylesheets and inline styles. Each method has its own advantages and trade-offs, making it essential for developers to choose the right approach based on their project requirements. Furthermore, implementing responsive design is crucial for creating user-friendly applications across devices. By leveraging techniques like media queries, CSS frameworks, and layout systems, developers can ensure that their applications are not only functional but also visually appealing on any screen size. As you continue to work with React, mastering these styling techniques will greatly enhance your ability to create engaging and responsive user interfaces.

Chapter 6: State Management

State management is a crucial aspect of developing React applications. Proper state management allows developers to maintain, access, and manipulate the application's state effectively, leading to a more predictable and maintainable codebase. In this chapter, we will explore state management concepts, focusing on the Context API and Redux, and how they enhance data flow and component interaction in React applications.

Introduction to State Management

What is State?

In React, **state** refers to a built-in object that holds dynamic data and controls the component's behavior. Unlike props, which are passed from parent to child components, state is managed internally within the component. Changes to the state can trigger a re-render of the component, allowing the UI to reflect the latest data.

Why State Management is Important

As applications grow in complexity, managing state can become challenging. When multiple components rely on the same state, the process of passing data through props can lead to "prop drilling," where data is passed down through many layers of components. This can make code hard to read and maintain. Effective state management solutions help to simplify data flow, making it easier to share state across components without convoluted prop structures.

Key Concepts

1. **Local State**: Managed within individual components. Suitable for UI-specific data that doesn't need to be shared.
2. **Global State**: Shared across multiple components. Requires a more sophisticated management approach to maintain consistency.
3. **Derived State**: State computed from other state values. While derived state can simplify logic, it should be used carefully to avoid unnecessary complexity.

Context API Overview

What is the Context API?

The **Context API** is a built-in feature of React that enables developers to share state across the component tree without explicitly passing props through every level. It provides a way to create global state that can be accessed by any component that needs it.

Creating Context

To use the Context API, you first need to create a context using `React.createContext()`:

```
import React, { createContext, useContext, useState } from 'react';

const MyContext = createContext();
```

Providing Context

Next, you provide the context to your component tree using a `Provider`. The `Provider` component makes the state available to any component that is a descendant in the tree

```
function MyProvider({ children }) {

  const [value, setValue] = useState("Hello, World!");

  return (

    <MyContext.Provider value={{ value, setValue }}>
```

```
    {children}

  </MyContext.Provider>

 );

}
```

Consuming Context

To access the context in a component, you use the `useContext` hook:

```
function MyComponent() {

  const { value, setValue } = useContext(MyContext);

  return (

    <div>  <p>{value}</p>

      <button onClick={() => setValue("Hello, React!")}>Change Message</button>

    </div>

  );

}
```

Benefits of the Context API

- **Avoids Prop Drilling**: Components can access state directly from the context, simplifying data sharing.
- **Easier Management**: It allows centralized state management for components that are far apart in the component tree.
- **Lightweight**: The Context API is built into React, requiring no additional libraries.

Limitations of the Context API

- **Performance**: Updating context can lead to re-renders in all consuming components, potentially impacting performance in larger applications.
- **Complexity**: For large-scale applications, the Context API can become difficult to manage. In such cases, other state management libraries may be more suitable.

Introduction to Redux

What is Redux?

Redux is a predictable state container for JavaScript applications. It is often used with React to manage global state more effectively. Redux follows three fundamental principles:

1. **Single Source of Truth**: The entire state of the application is stored in a single object (the store), making it easier to track changes.
2. **State is Read-Only**: The only way to change the state is by dispatching actions, ensuring that state changes are traceable.
3. **Changes are Made with Pure Functions**: State updates are handled by reducers, which are pure functions that take the previous state and an action as arguments and return a new state.

Setting Up Redux

To use Redux in a React application, you typically need to install the Redux and React-Redux libraries:

npm install redux react-redux

Creating a Store

First, you create a Redux store using `createStore`:

import { createStore } from 'redux';

const initialState = {

  message: "Hello, Redux!"

};

```
const reducer = (state = initialState, action) => {
  switch (action.type) {
    case 'CHANGE_MESSAGE':
      return { ...state, message: action.payload };
    default:
      return state;
  }
};


const store = createStore(reducer);
```

Providing the Store

Next, you provide the store to your application using the `Provider` component from React-Redux:

```
import { Provider } from 'react-redux';

function App() {
  return (
```

```jsx
    <Provider store={store}>
      <MyComponent />
    </Provider>
  );
}
```

Dispatching Actions

To change the state, you dispatch actions:

```jsx
const changeMessage = (newMessage) => ({
  type: 'CHANGE_MESSAGE',
  payload: newMessage,
});


// In a component
dispatch(changeMessage("Hello, Redux World!"));
```

Accessing State

To access the state in a component, you can use the `useSelector` hook:

import { useSelector } from 'react-redux';

function MyComponent() {

  const message = useSelector(state => state.message);

  return <p>{message}</p>;

}

Benefits of Redux

- **Predictability**: With a single source of truth and strict guidelines for state changes, applications become more predictable and easier to debug.
- **Debugging Tools**: Redux DevTools provides a powerful way to inspect actions, state changes, and the application's history.
- **Middleware Support**: Redux supports middleware, allowing for powerful asynchronous actions and side effects

management (e.g., with Redux Thunk or Redux Saga).

Limitations of Redux

- **Boilerplate Code**: Redux can introduce a lot of boilerplate code, especially for small applications.
- **Learning Curve**: The concepts of actions, reducers, and the store can be complex for beginners.

Chapter 7: React Router

React Router is a powerful library for managing navigation in single-page applications (SPAs). It allows developers to create a dynamic, responsive routing system that enhances the user experience.

Understanding Single Page Applications (SPAs)

What is a Single Page Application?

A **Single Page Application (SPA)** is a web application that loads a single HTML page and dynamically updates the content as the user interacts with the app. This contrasts with traditional multi-page applications that reload the entire page when navigating.

Benefits of SPAs

1. **Improved User Experience**: SPAs provide a smooth and fast experience by updating only parts of the page without a full reload.
2. **Reduced Server Load**: Since SPAs only load resources once, they can reduce the number of requests made to the server.

3. **Client-Side Routing**: SPAs enable client-side routing, allowing users to navigate through the application without experiencing full page transitions.

Setting Up React Router

Installing React Router

To use React Router, you need to install it:

npm install react-router-dom

Basic Setup

Once installed, you can set up routing in your application by wrapping your components with the `BrowserRouter` component:

import { BrowserRouter as Router, Route, Switch } from 'react-router-dom';

function App() {

  return (

```
    <Router>
      <Switch>
        <Route path="/" exact component={Home} />
        <Route path="/about" component={About} />
        <Route path="/contact" component={Contact} />
      </Switch>
    </Router>
  );
}
```

Understanding `Route` and `Switch`

- **Route**: The `Route` component renders a specified component based on the current URL path. The `exact` prop ensures that the route matches the URL exactly.
- **Switch**: The `Switch` component renders the first matching `Route` and ignores the rest. This is useful for managing multiple routes.

Navigation and Route Parameters

Navigating Between Routes

To navigate between routes, you can use the `Link` component:

```
import { Link } from 'react-router-dom';
```

```
function Navbar() {
  return (
    <nav>
      <Link to="/">Home</Link>
      <Link to="/about">About</Link>
      <Link to="/contact">Contact</Link>
    </nav>
  );
}
```

Route Parameters

React Router also allows for dynamic routing using route parameters. This is useful for scenarios like displaying user profiles based on their IDs.

Example of Route Parameters:

```
<Route path="/user/:id" component={UserProfile} />
```

In the `UserProfile` component, you can access the `id` parameter using the `useParams` hook:

```
import { useParams } from 'react-router-dom';

function UserProfile() {
  const { id } = useParams();

  return <h1>User ID: {id}</h1>;
}
```

Nested Routes

React Router supports nested routing, allowing you to render child routes inside parent routes. This is useful for organizing related components.

Example of Nested Routes:

<Route path="/dashboard">

  <Dashboard>

    <Route path="settings" component={Settings} />

    <Route path="profile" component={Profile} />

  </Dashboard>

</Route>

In this setup, the `Dashboard` component can render either the `Settings` or `Profile` component based on the nested route.

Conclusion

We examined React Router, a powerful library for managing navigation in single-page applications. By leveraging React Router, developers can create dynamic, user-friendly experiences with seamless navigation. Together, effective state management and routing are fundamental for building robust React applications that provide excellent user experiences. As you continue to develop your React skills, mastering these topics will significantly enhance your ability to create interactive, responsive applications.

Chapter 8: Fetching Data

Fetching data is a crucial aspect of building modern web applications, and in React, it plays a significant role in ensuring dynamic and interactive user experiences. This chapter delves into the key concepts of API calls, the tools for fetching data, and how to handle asynchronous operations in React.

Introduction to API Calls

API calls are essential for accessing and manipulating data from external sources. An API (Application Programming Interface) serves as a bridge between your application and the data you want to retrieve or send. When working with web applications, most data comes from remote servers via APIs.

Types of APIs:

- **REST APIs:** These use standard HTTP methods (GET, POST, PUT, DELETE) to interact with resources, making them a common choice for web applications.
- **GraphQL:** A more flexible alternative to REST, GraphQL allows clients to request only the data they need, reducing the amount of data transferred over the network.

- **WebSocket APIs**: Suitable for real-time applications, WebSockets enable two-way communication between the server and client.

Understanding how to make API calls is fundamental for fetching data, whether it's for displaying user profiles, fetching product details, or interacting with third-party services.

Using Fetch and Axios

In JavaScript, there are several methods to make API calls. The two most popular ones are the native `Fetch API` and the third-party library `Axios`.

Using Fetch: The Fetch API provides a simple way to make network requests. It's promise-based, which makes it suitable for modern JavaScript applications. Here's a basic example:

import axios from 'axios';

axios.get('https://api.example.com/data')

  .then(response => console.log(response.data))

  .catch(error => console.error('Axios error:', error));

Using Axios can often lead to cleaner and more readable code, especially when dealing with complex API interactions.

Handling Async Operations in React

When fetching data in React, you must handle asynchronous operations carefully to ensure that the UI remains responsive. React provides several hooks, particularly `useEffect` and `useState`, to manage these operations effectively.

Using useEffect: The `useEffect` hook is used to perform side effects in function components, such as fetching data. It can be set to run once on component mount or when specific dependencies change. Here's an example of fetching data inside a functional component:

import React, { useState, useEffect } from 'react';

import axios from 'axios';

const DataFetchingComponent = () => {

  const [data, setData] = useState([]);

  const [loading, setLoading] = useState(true);

  const [error, setError] = useState(null);

```
useEffect(() => {

  const fetchData = async () => {

    try {

      const response = await axios.get('https://api.example.com/data');

      setData(response.data);

    } catch (err) {

      setError(err);

    } finally {

      setLoading(false);

    }

  };


  fetchData();

}, []); // Empty dependency array means this runs once on mount
```

```
if (loading) return <p>Loading...</p>;

if (error) return <p>Error: {error.message}</p>;


return (
  <div>
    {data.map(item => (
      <div key={item.id}>{item.name}</div>
    ))}
  </div>
 );
};
```

In this example, we:

- Use `useState` to manage the `data`, `loading`, and `error` states.
- Use `useEffect` to call the `fetchData` function when the component mounts.
- Handle loading and error states to provide feedback to users.

Error Handling: Proper error handling is crucial when dealing with asynchronous operations. In the example above, errors are caught in the `catch` block, and we update the state to reflect the error. This practice ensures that users are informed about issues that may arise during data fetching.

Cleanup: If your component may unmount while an API call is in progress (e.g., if it's part of a route that the user navigates away from), it's good practice to handle cleanup. This can be done by tracking a mounted state to prevent trying to update the state of an unmounted component:

```
useEffect(() => {

  let isMounted = true;


  const fetchData = async () => {

    try {

      const response = await axios.get('https://api.example.com/data');

      if (isMounted) {

        setData(response.data);

      }
```

```
      } catch (err) {
        if (isMounted) {
          setError(err);
        }
      } finally {
        if (isMounted) {
          setLoading(false);
        }
      }
    };

    fetchData();
    return () => {
      isMounted = false; // Cleanup on unmount
    };
  }, []);
```

This pattern helps avoid memory leaks and ensures that your application behaves correctly even if the user navigates away before the data is fetched.

Conclusion

Fetching data in React applications involves making API calls, handling asynchronous operations, and managing state. Whether using the Fetch API or Axios, it's essential to understand how to perform these tasks effectively to create responsive and user-friendly applications. Proper error handling and cleanup are also critical to maintaining application stability and performance. By mastering these concepts, you can enhance the interactivity and robustness of your React applications.

Chapter 9: Testing React Applications

Importance of Testing

Testing is a fundamental practice in software development, crucial for ensuring that applications function as intended and maintain high quality. In the context of React applications, testing provides several benefits:

1. **Bug Detection**: Early identification of bugs helps reduce the cost and effort involved in fixing issues later in the development cycle. Automated tests can quickly pinpoint where a problem lies.
2. **Code Quality**: Writing tests encourages developers to write cleaner, more modular code. When components are designed with testability in mind, they tend to be easier to understand and maintain.
3. **Refactoring Confidence**: When making changes or optimizations to existing code, having a suite of tests gives developers confidence that their modifications won't introduce new bugs.
4. **Documentation**: Well-written tests serve as documentation for how components should behave. They provide a clear understanding of the expected inputs and outputs, making it

easier for new developers to grasp the functionality.
5. **Improved Collaboration**: With automated tests, team members can work on different parts of the codebase simultaneously. If changes are made, tests ensure that existing functionality is not broken, enhancing team collaboration.

Introduction to Jest and React Testing Library

To effectively test React applications, developers commonly use tools like Jest and the React Testing Library (RTL).

Jest is a powerful testing framework developed by Facebook. It provides an extensive suite of features, including:

- **Zero configuration**: Jest works out of the box with minimal setup, especially when using Create React App.
- **Built-in mocking**: Jest includes capabilities for mocking functions and modules, allowing for isolated testing of components.
- **Snapshot testing**: This feature enables developers to capture the rendered output of a component and compare it with future outputs to catch unexpected changes.
- **Test coverage**: Jest can generate reports on test coverage, helping identify parts of the codebase that lack adequate testing.

React Testing Library is designed to facilitate testing React components in a way that mimics how users interact with them. It promotes best practices by encouraging developers to test components based on user behavior rather than implementation details. This leads to more reliable tests and better user experiences.

Key Features of React Testing Library:

- **Querying elements**: RTL provides various queries to find elements in the DOM, such as `getByText`, `getByRole`, and `getByPlaceholderText`. These queries prioritize accessibility and user experience.
- **User events**: RTL integrates with user-event library to simulate user interactions, allowing tests to reflect real-world usage.

Writing Unit Tests for Components

Unit tests focus on testing individual components in isolation. Here's a step-by-step approach to writing unit tests for React components using Jest and React Testing Library.

1. Setting Up the Test Environment: Most React projects created with Create React App come with Jest and RTL configured. To create a test file, simply create a file with the `.test.js` extension in the same directory as the component you want to test.

2. Writing Tests: Let's consider a simple `Button` component. Here's how you might write tests for it:

Button Component:

import React from 'react';

const Button = ({ onClick, text }) => {

  return (

    <button onClick={onClick}>

      {text}

    </button>

  );

};

export default Button;

Button.test.js:

import React from 'react';

import { render, screen, fireEvent } from '@testing-library/react';

```javascript
import Button from './Button';

describe('Button Component', () => {

  test('renders with correct text', () => {

    render(<Button text="Click Me" />);

    const buttonElement = screen.getByText(/click me/i);

    expect(buttonElement).toBeInTheDocument();

  });

  test('calls onClick function when clicked', () => {

    const handleClick = jest.fn();

    render(<Button text="Click Me" onClick={handleClick} />);

    const buttonElement = screen.getByText(/click me/i);

    fireEvent.click(buttonElement);

    expect(handleClick).toHaveBeenCalledTimes(1);

  });

});
```

3. Running Tests: You can run your tests using the command:

npm test

Jest will watch for changes and run the tests accordingly. You can also run specific tests or generate coverage reports.

4. Best Practices:

- **Focus on User Behavior**: Write tests that reflect how users will interact with your components rather than their internal implementation.
- **Keep Tests Isolated**: Each test should focus on a single behavior or aspect of the component to ensure clarity and maintainability.
- **Mock External Dependencies**: When components rely on external APIs or libraries, use Jest's mocking capabilities to isolate the tests and prevent dependencies from affecting outcomes.

Chapter 10: Building and Deploying Your Application

Preparing for Production

Before deploying your React application, it's vital to prepare it for production. This involves optimizing performance and ensuring security. Key steps include:

1. **Minification**: Minifying JavaScript and CSS files reduces their size by removing whitespace, comments, and unnecessary characters, which improves loading times.
2. **Tree Shaking**: Modern bundlers like Webpack eliminate unused code (dead code elimination) from your production build. Ensure your code is modular to benefit from this feature.
3. **Code Splitting**: This technique allows you to split your application into smaller chunks, which can be loaded on demand. This reduces the initial load time of your application.
4. **Environment Variables**: Use environment variables to configure settings specific to your production environment, such as API URLs and feature flags. You can set these in

a `.env` file, and React will pick them up during the build process.
5. **Security Measures**: Review your application for common security issues, such as XSS (Cross-Site Scripting) and CSRF (Cross-Site Request Forgery). Use libraries like `helmet` to set HTTP headers that enhance security.

Building Your React Application

To create a production-ready build of your React application, you typically run the following command:

npm run build

This command triggers the build process, which generates an optimized version of your application in the `build` directory. The output includes:

- An `index.html` file as the entry point for your app.
- A `static` folder containing minified JavaScript and CSS files.
- Source maps for debugging, which can be disabled in production if necessary.

The build process leverages Webpack under the hood, optimizing your assets and preparing them for deployment.

Deployment Options

Once your application is built, you have various options for deployment, each with its own advantages and considerations:

1. **Static Hosting**: Services like **Netlify**, **Vercel**, and **GitHub Pages** are ideal for hosting static sites. They provide easy integration with Git repositories for continuous deployment. Simply push your code, and these platforms automatically deploy your latest build.
2. **Cloud Services**: Platforms like **AWS**, **Google Cloud**, and **Azure** offer flexible deployment options. You can use services like AWS S3 for static file hosting, AWS Lambda for serverless functions, or container orchestration with Kubernetes.
3. **Traditional Web Servers**: If you need more control, you can deploy your application on
4. traditional web servers like **Nginx** or **Apache**. This approach requires configuring your server to serve static files and set up reverse proxies if necessary.
5. **Serverless Functions**: For applications requiring backend functionality, consider using serverless platforms such as **AWS**

Lambda or **Firebase Functions**. These services allow you to deploy backend code without managing server infrastructure, scaling automatically based on demand.

6. **Containerization**: Tools like **Docker** enable you to package your application and its dependencies into containers. This ensures consistency across development, testing, and production environments. You can deploy these containers to cloud services or orchestration platforms.

Choosing the Right Option: The best deployment option depends on your application's architecture, requirements, and your team's familiarity with the tools. Consider factors like scalability, cost, and ease of setup when making your decision.

Conclusion

Testing and deployment are critical phases in the development of React applications. Testing ensures that your components work as intended and maintain quality over time, while a well-planned deployment process guarantees that your application reaches users efficiently and securely. By leveraging tools like Jest and React Testing Library for testing, and understanding various deployment options, you can build robust, reliable applications that meet user expectations and perform well in production.

Summary

Recap of Key Concepts

Throughout this exploration of React, we've covered essential concepts that form the backbone of effective React application development. We began with the foundational elements of React, including components, props, and state management, which enable developers to create interactive and dynamic user interfaces. We then delved into fetching data, highlighting the importance of APIs and the tools available, such as the Fetch API and Axios. Understanding how to handle asynchronous operations with hooks like `useEffect` was crucial for managing data flow.

Testing emerged as a vital practice, underscoring the importance of quality assurance in software development. Tools like Jest and React Testing Library facilitate unit testing, ensuring components function as expected and fostering maintainability. Finally, we discussed the build and deployment processes, emphasizing the significance of preparing applications for production and exploring various deployment options to effectively deliver applications to users.

Next Steps in Your React Journey

As you continue your journey with React, consider diving deeper into advanced topics such as state management libraries (like Redux or Context API), routing with React Router, and performance optimization techniques. Exploring TypeScript with React can also enhance your skills by adding type safety to your components.

Building real-world projects is one of the best ways to solidify your understanding. Try contributing to open-source projects, or create your own applications that address personal interests or real-world problems.

Additional Resources

Recommended Books and Courses:

- **Books**:
    - *"React - The Complete Guide"* by Maximilian Schwarzmüller: A comprehensive resource covering React from basics to advanced concepts.
    - *"Learning React"* by Alex Banks and Eve Porcello: A beginner-friendly guide that provides a solid foundation in React.
- **Courses**:
    - **Udemy**: Look for courses by reputable instructors focusing on React, often with hands-on projects.
    - **Pluralsight**: Offers structured learning paths for React and related technologies.

Online Communities and Forums:

- **Stack Overflow**: A great platform to ask questions and find solutions related to React development.
- **Reddit**: Subreddits like r/reactjs offer discussions, resources, and support from fellow developers.
- **Discord and Slack Communities**: Join channels dedicated to React to connect with other learners and professionals for real-time discussions.

Engaging with these resources and communities can enhance your learning experience, keeping you updated with the latest trends and best practices in the React ecosystem. Embrace continuous learning, and enjoy your journey in becoming a proficient React developer!

www.ingramcontent.com/pod-product-compliance
Lightning Source LLC
Chambersburg PA
CBHW070111230526
45472CB00004B/1212